Zeal for God's House Quickened
by Oliver Bowles
with chapters by C. Matthew McMahon

Copyright Information

Zeal for God's House Quickened, by Oliver Bowles, with chapters by C. Matthew McMahon, Ph.D., Th.D.

Edited by Therese B. McMahon

© 2020 by Puritan Publications and A Puritan's Mind

Published by Puritan Publications
A Ministry of A Puritan's Mind in Crossville, TN
www.apuritansmind.com
www.puritanpublications.com

All rights reserved. No part of this publication may be reproduced, stored in a retrieval system or transmitted in any form by any means, electronic, mechanical, photocopy, recording or otherwise, without the prior permission of the publisher, except as provided by USA copyright law.

First Electronic Edition, 2020
First Modern Print Edition, 2020
Manufactured in the United States of America

eISBN: 978-1-62663-382-7
ISBN: 978-1-62663-383-4

Cover Art: Westminster Abbey

Table of Contents

Spurious Faith and False Zeal - McMahon 4
Meet Oliver Bowles - McMahon 13
Imprimatur 16
Preface 18
PART 1: The Text Opened 25
PART 2: Defining Zeal 31
PART 3: The Doctrine 33
PART 4: Zeal in Church Reformation 36
PART 5: Zeal in Reformers 58
PART 6: How Zeal Must Be Qualified 61
PART 7: Uses to Reformers 64
PART 8: The Best Way to be Zealous in Preaching . 86
Other Works by Westminster Divines on Reformation Published by Puritan Publications 95

Spurious Faith and False Zeal
by C. Matthew McMahon, Ph.D. Th.D.

"And seeing a fig tree afar off having leaves, he came, if haply he might find any thing thereon: and when he came to it, he found nothing but leaves," (Mark 11:13).

If the outward performance of religious zeal stems from the inward change wrought by the Holy Spirit, then such action is of divine grace – it is supernatural. The motioning of the Spirit of God on one of the elect saints aimed at the glorification of Christ through godly piety is commanded, encouraged and praised. Every Christian church should be filled to the uttermost with professing Christians who are taking heaven by storm, violently seizing the Kingdom of God by force, and pressing into it with all their might (Matthew 11:12; Luke 16:16), all with *a display of godly zeal.* But if what appears to be good, like a fruitful fig tree spied from afar with fruit bearing leaves, is actually a bad tree, hypocrisy in false zeal without repentance? It will be damning to the individual, and hurtful to the church.

Though there are those who glorify Christ in their religious zeal through obedience to the revealed word, there are also those who perform external religious acts though they remain unconverted (Matthew 23:23-24). Those who are living under the eminent means of grace but possess a superficial affection to the things of God often harm the church most of all (Jeremiah 7:4). They introduce a form of godliness *but deny the power of God*, (2 Tim. 3:5). And what is this but the *natural man* corrupting the work of the Spirit in the lives of the congregation?

Saul of Tarsus, before he was converted, persecuted the church beyond measure. He was such a wicked man before his conversion, that when he desired to join himself to the church, as it is recorded in Acts 9:26, that he was rejected by the disciples due to his former lifestyle. "And when Saul was come to Jerusalem, he assayed to join himself to the disciples, but they were all afraid of him, and believed not that he was a disciple."[1] There was no difficulty perceiving his unjust and cruel tactics against the church while he remained unconverted. But what about a zeal towards a godly life? The disciples were *careful* in their inclusion of individuals in the church to see if such zeal for godliness

---

[1] This ought to inform Christian churches something about the manner in which they form their membership values, or lack thereof.

was apparent. It is somewhat easy for wickedness in blatant forms to be clearly distinguished and noticed, especially when it comes from outside the church as in this case with Saul, or in the case of the Pharisees against the preaching of Christ's disciples. But what shall be said of a kind of *religious zeal* which looks, walks, talks and acts as a Christian, but in reality, is not Christian?

When religious zeal is clouded in ignorance, though it is coupled in good intentions, the well-being of the church will be compromised. *Good and excited intentions* do not breed regenerated Christians. The affect of unregenerate and ignorant religious zealots has a profoundly negative affect on the church.[2] Certainly, those who persecute the church from without are much more easily distinguishable, as stated above in the case of Paul, than those in the church. Speaking about himself, Paul states in Philippians 3:6 that he was *thoroughly zealous* in persecuting the church while unconverted, "Concerning zeal, persecuting the church..." Paul also remarks in Romans 10:2 that the Jews were exceedingly religious in their *zeal* for God though they remained unconverted. They were without

---

[2] *Historical Theology* bears this out greatly. See my work on that subject, *Historical Theology Made Easy*.

saving knowledge though they believed they were serving God, "For I bear them record that they have a zeal of God, but not according to knowledge." This teaches us that people can be religious, and zealous for that religion, though have no conception of what constitutes *true religion to the glory of Jesus Christ.*

The unregenerate religious zealot may be almost anyone in the church. This statement is qualified by the definition of "unregenerate religious zealot." It must be noted that these people are *religiously* zealous. That means they have a *form* of godliness about them in the external works they perform in the church, in their home, and at their work. They are taken up in a religious fanaticism, which may sometimes, pass itself off as true Christianity. They are *perceived* as real Christians by real Christians. In this way, the religious zealot may be one of the *pastors* of the church, a deacon, a board member, a husband, a wife, or any of the children. The plague of false religious zeal does not infect one particular class or age of people in the church. It is not restricted to dark-haired males ages 30-35. False religious zeal may infect anyone who does not possess the life-changing power of the Holy Spirit resting in the bosom of their soul (John 3:3-5).

In the parable of the sower, Jesus teaches us that any seed which is sown, and springs up quickly, does not last. As a matter of fact, it withers away and dies because it has no root. In Matthew 13:5-6 he explains the planting and growth of this kind of seed, "Some fell upon stony places where they had not much earth; and forthwith they sprung up, because they had not deepness of earth: and when the sun was up they were scorched; and because they had no root, they withered away." This is deemed "spurious faith." Spurious faith comes from *newly* planted seeds. These are new converts. It may be characterized by a faith which springs up and desires *to change the world* for King Jesus with great ardor right out of the gate. This is the trademark of the religious zealot. But this type of spurious faith does not ultimately last. It springs up, grows for a time, then the sun scorches it and it ultimately dies. It is fervent about working for the Kingdom *for a time* (however long or short that may be) but then ultimately will be hard pressed by the world and its temptations and sin, and finally drawn away to apostacy.

Spurious faith is not Christian faith at all. It is a faith which is man-made, based on the excitement of the moment, or the apprehension of some doctrine which stirs the empty soul for a time. The religious vacuum inside every heart longs for something expressly religious to fill it up. These kinds of hearts are *always* in danger of spurious faith. If such a faith is possessed by a *pastor*, as Mr. Bowles will warn the Assembly in the ensuing discourse, it may be continually cultivated for a time, even a period of years, being fed with new ideas from the Word of God as the unconverted pastor studies each week. Yet even in this, to *himself*, his ministry remains spiritually unfruitful. Though he has something new to say, though he may be quite sincere in his profession of faith, and though he may be an apt theologian and teacher, such a faith will ultimately wither and dry up (and that often over a longer period of time for such people). Here is where Christians may view saints which appear to be like pillars to the church, crumble and fall into "apostasy." The opposite to false zeal, is godly and biblical zeal, one which strives for a thorough biblical reformation, and gives birth to true reformers, true reformation for the glory of Christ, which is the substance of Bowles' work.

    Mr. Bowles, in this excellent and stirring treatise, is addressing the Westminster Divines (to keep in its context) in their vigilant care for the common good of the church. He is fighting diligently against *false* zeal, *hypocritical* zeal, or even a *lack* of zeal. The Assembly had been called together to set down God's truth as it concerns the settling of doctrine, worship, and church government for the good of Christ's people. But in what *method and manner* should they set down such eternally important truths? As Bowles explains from John 2:17, "And his disciples remembered that it was written, "The zeal of thy house hath eaten me up,"" *zeal* is the manner that they must do all things for the glory of God. It is a hearty soul-work, for without true biblical zeal, there is *no pleasing service* rendered to the Christ. What will a cold, lazy, indifferent reformer accomplish? What would *a group* of cold, lazy, indifferent reformers ever accomplish?

Annexed to this inspiring word on enacting zealous reformation, and setting down the character and work of zealous reformers, Bowles shows how church-reformation is a work of the largest extent, as that which concerns *all* professing churches, whose eternal happiness or misery will be the outcome of either exercising biblical zeal for the glory of God, or not. For biblical zeal, as it mimics the Lord Jesus Christ, is a holy ardor kindled by the Holy Spirit of God in the affections, improving a man to the utmost for God's glory, and the church's good; and it is without a doubt that church reformation calls for utmost zeal.

Though Bowles spoke to the Assembly in this sermon, he took time, afterwards, to, as he said, "make bold a supply of that which at the time of the delivery he could not do." So, this work is the *expanded* piece, taken from that original sermon, which he added to and enlarged (quite a bit). It is not that this, now treatise, is solely for the historical assembly, but *all* that would take up the mantle of reformation for the glory of Christ's church. He covers what zeal is in church reform, over and against false zeal; how zeal is manifested in true reformers, what practical aspects zeal plays for the work of reformation, and then gives some uses to the doctrine. His word to preachers as reformers, the concluding section of the work, is something *every preacher should hear.* That preachers who desire to see Christ's church flourish under the work of the Spirit ought to take up preaching that is zealous, compassionate, convincing (with conviction), sensible to the needs of the people, as frequent as possible, and with all gravity, to the glory of God and the good of the saints.

May you be blessed and inspired by Bowles as you reject false zeal, and take to heart true, biblical zeal.

In the blessings of Christ,
C. Matthew McMahon, Ph.D., Th.D.
From my study, September, 2020.

Meet Oliver Bowles
Edited by C. Matthew McMahon

Oliver Bowles (1574-1664?)[3] B.D. was one of the oldest members of the Westminster Assembly, a learned scholar, a celebrated tutor[4] and a man of great piety. This esteemed divine was fellow of Queen's college, Cambridge, where he most probably received his education. After leaving the university, he became preacher of Sutton in Bedfordshire, around the year 1607, where he continued for fifty years.

Bowles was chosen one of the Westminster Assembly of Divines, where he constantly attended, and was very useful in that learned company. The assembly, having petitioned the parliament for a fast, previous to its entering on the business of setting down a uniform confession for all the Reformed Churches, Mr. Bowles and Mr. Matthew Newcomen were appointed to preach before both houses and the assembly, and both sermons were ordered to be published.

Mr. Bowles's work entitled, "Zeal for God's House Quickened; or, a Sermon preached before the

---

[3] If Bowles was born in 1574, and died at ninety, he would have lived to 1664. But his dates are disputed.
[4] The famous Dr. Preston was one of his pupils.

Assembly of Lords, Commons, and Divines, at their solemn Fast," July 7, 1643, in Abbey Church, Westminster: expresses zeal required in Church-Reformers. Mr. Bowles was author of a work entitled, "De Pastore Evangelico," which surrounds the Gospel ministry, (1649). Dr. Calamy describes this book as excellent. It was published by his son, and dedicated to the Earl of Manchester. He adds, that it was "a book not suffered to creep out in the time of the rampant episcopacy, not for any evil there is in it, but because some men do not care to be put upon too much work."

Though Mr. Bowles survived the restoration many years it does not appear either to have conformed or to have been ejected; but, on account of his great age, and for several other reasons, there is the strongest probability to suppose that he finished preaching about the year 1659 or 1660. He calmly resigned his soul into the hands of his dear Redeemer, September 5, 1674, supposed to be upwards of ninety years of age.[5]

Bowles had twelve sons, one of which was an ejected nonconformist.

The excellent Mr. Timothy Cruso was favored with the friendship and counsel of Mr. Bowles. He

---

[5] See footnote 2.

attended him during his last illness, and received the following affectionate advice from him the day before his death. "Have a care of yourself, Timothy, in this evil world; and be not so entangled with the vanities of it as to lose the substance for the shadow. Seeing you design yourself for the work and office of the ministry, I would advise you never to trouble your hearers with useless or contending notions but rather preach all practically, that you may set them upon doing, and more advance a holy life. I would not any longer live that idle and unserviceable life which I have lately done; and therefore if God had some work for me yet to do here, he will continue me yet here: but if not I am sure there is better work for me in heaven, by which I shall act for his praise and glory more."

"When I took my last leave of him," Mr. Cruso says, he said, "Farewell Timothy; and if I see thee not any more in this world, (as indeed he did not,) I hope I shall in the next, which is better!" and so I hope also, replied Mr. Cruso. "Only remember," continued Mr. Bowles," to keep a good conscience, and walk closely with God." These last words he twice repeated with considerable emphasis, that it might make a deeper impression on his mind.

Imprimatur[6]

Die Iovis. July 27, 1643.

To the Right Honorable the House of Lords, and the Honorable House of Commons, Assembled in Parliament, and to the Learned and Religious Divines called by them, and now assembled to consult about matters of Religion.

Zeal for God's House Quickened: or, a sermon preached before the Assembly of Lords, Commons, and Divines, at their solemn fast July 7, 1643. In the abbey church at Westminster.

Expressing the eminency of Zeal requisite in Church Reformers, by Oliver Bowles, Pastor of Sutton in Bedfordshire.

---

[6] *Zeal for God's House Quickened*: or, A sermon preached before the assembly of Lords, Commons, and Divines, at their solemn fast July 7, 1643, in the Abbey Church at Westminster. Expressing the eminency of zeal requisite in church reformers; by Oliver Bowles, Pastor of Sutton in Bedfordshire. Published by order of both Houses of Parliament.

"It is good to be zealously affected always in a good thing," (Gal. 4:18).

Published by Order of both Houses of Parliament.

(London: Printed by Richard Bishop for Samuel Gellibrand, at the Brazen Serpent in Pauls Church-yard, 1643).

It is this day ordered by the Lords in Parliament, that Mr. Bowles has hereby thanks given to him, for the great pains he took in the sermon he made at the Fast for the Assembly of Divines in the Abbey Church, Westminster, on Friday the seventh of this month of July. And is hereby desired to cause his said sermon to be forthwith *printed and published.*

Jo. Brown Cler. Parliamentor.

Preface

Right honorable and most worthy,

    Out of your vigilant care for the common good you have found out a way amidst your many distractions to convene an Assembly of grave and learned Divines, with whom you might advise concerning the settling of doctrine, worship, and church government.

    You saw cause which might move you so to do in respect; first, of those licentious spirits, who took occasion, as to vent their own imaginations, so to attempt anything in matter of doctrine and worship. Secondly, in that for lack of an established Church-government, we were and still are in danger to fall from a tyranny to an anarchy. Thirdly, in that evil-minded men, seeing no effectual means provided to suppress such variety of sects started up, were ready to censure you, as those who favored such opinions. What you have done, has been done with much prudence in that you have given way for the admittance of Divines of different judgements to be chosen, to whom a liberty is not denied to plead in every one's own party. And not only so, but you have further embodied diverse of your *worthy ones* of both Houses, as *members* of our Assembly. By this privilege, we have many and singular advantages. When this Assembly, for the greater part, was by your summons gathered together, you were pleased, out of a due consideration of the weighty affairs to be transacted, to appoint a Solemn Fast to be kept (chiefly) by the Members of the Assembly. And when you had so done, your pleasure was to lay your command on myself, though the unworthiest of many, to be employed in the service of that day. Surely, it was not but that you had your choice of many other most able and worthy Divines, only it was your pleasure, that days and multitudes of years should speak.

    The grace I chose as most necessary to treat of, was that of zeal, as conversant about *God's House*. First, for that it directly opposes luke-warmness, the most dangerous and yet the epidemic disease of our time. Secondly, for no one grace more than zeal promotes the work of Reformation, (as will appear in the subsequent discourse). Thirdly, for that among all other ornaments, there is none that more beautifies a reformer in the eyes of God and man than zeal. This is a proverb, "There are many creatures," said the wise man, "that are comely in there going; but none so comely as *a zealous reformer.*"

Preface

Accordingly, then (you Parliamentary Worthies) go on and prosper, do not cease to carry on your work, which is God's work, with zeal and courage. It is perseverance alone that will both crown you, and perfect your endeavors. What encouragement you have had, in that the Lord, amidst your greatest dangers, has been mightily seen in the protection of your persons! No weapons of war that have been formed against you have prospered; the tongues of men that have risen up in judgement against you, he has condemned. Has not the same God assisted you to do many glorious works, by which his name has been honored, and his people unspeakably benefitted? How has the Lord kept you together until this day! Notwithstanding the endeavors of all the devils in hell, and wicked men on earth, to scatter you, and to divide you! What a foundation has the Lord laid of your continuance together until your work is done! Surely, it is that he has yet some great things for you to do. If you (which God forbid) shall faint, and withdraw yourselves from the service, be sure that God without you will accomplish his work, but tremble to think what will become of you and yours. How much would it be a thing to be bewailed that you (Noble and brave spirited Patriots; who have here born the heat of the day, the brunt of the business, so far denied yourselves, as to risk all that you are, have, or might expect) should now by failing in your last act, loose your crown, forfeit your reward from God and man!

And now for you, (my Reverend and much Honored Brethren in the common work of the ministry), who can but bless the Lord, for that degree of his Spirit, (no doubt, it is the effect, as of your own prayers in the day of your solemn humiliation, so of many of the prayers of his people), which he has showered down on you! Not only do your learned debates, your exact and judicious Scripture-discussions, your scholastic disputes, the discovery many of you have made of your exact knowledge in antiquity, show that God is among you, as he that has fitted you for the work. But also, further, your sweet amicable converse, your following of the truth in love, your differences in judgement carried on without alienation of affection, do not they all say that God is with you? God forbid, that either the devil, or wicked men, should break apart that sweet bond of amity, which with God has linked you into one. Be encouraged, then, (dearly beloved in the Lord) from one whom God was pleased, though the unworthiest among you, yet to make his preaching to you, to go on as carried along with a Spirit of indefatigable zeal in the pursuance of the work you are called to.

Behold *zeal* is soul-work, and that of nearest concern that God has put into your hands to be transacted. Is not your work a counter-work to that great and long plotted design, by which Popery should have been re-advanced, God's saving truth been suppressed, his worship substantially corrupted, and utterly destroyed? Is it not a work of the largest extent, as that which concerns all other Reformed Churches, whose happiness or misery will be involved in ours? Yes, ages to come will either bless or curse you, as you shall follow or neglect the opportunity.

And now for myself, be pleased to take notice that my strength and voice failing me by reason of my weakness, I have made bold to make a supply of that which at the time of the delivery I could not enlarge. Further, (this being a fixed rule to me, that God's Word should in preaching have the preeminence,) do not wonder, that I allege authors, in such cases in which their allegation does not prejudice Scripture. As first, when an historical truth is to be made good; for though the Scriptures do only determine, *Quid verum, quid falsum*, what is true and what false, yet for the information of ourselves, *Quid novum, quid antiquum,* we must have recourse to the writings of men. Secondly, if God himself, when he would shame men for their evils, sends them to learn from the creatures, (Jer. 10:6; Prov. 6; 1 Cor. 1:12-14) why may not we send men living in the days of light to learn of darker times? Thirdly, when being to reprove the evils of the time, for removing prejudice, we deliver our reproofs rather in the words of Antiquity than in our own.[7] So the Papists embraced many things in the writings of the fathers as Catholic, which they condemned in Luther as heretical.

    And now what remains but that we all humbly pray the God of all truth and peace, who alone is able to facilitate all difficulties, to direct and guide you, Honorable Senators, to pour on you that Spirit of wisdom and courage, that you may go with a settled resolution, never to give over, until you have established truth and peace in our borders; and the same God magnify his power in our weakness, and multiply the gifts of his Spirit on us, whom you have been pleased to call together, to advise with in the great affairs of the Church, that we may so discharge our duties, that God

---

[7] Facil patimur reprehensores qui remotiori feculo vixare.

may have glory, and his people the good that they expect and pray for, and all your enemies may have their faces covered with shame,

So prays your servant in the Lord,
OLIVER BOWLES.

PART 1: The Text Opened

John 2:17, "And his disciples remembered that it was written, "The zeal of thy house hath eaten me up.""

The prophet Malachi, prophesying concerning the Lord Christ, that he should in due time come to visit his church, sets him out as a Refiner, as a Purifier of silver, tells us that he should purify in special the son of Levi, purge them as gold and silver, (Mal. 3:3) that they might offer to the Lord an offering in righteousness. And as an accomplishment of this prophecy, the same Lord Christ gives a specimen, in the narrative immediately preceding my text, by his heroic fact of whipping the buyers and sellers out of the Temple (an evil which the priests for their gain had cemented.) I call it a heroic act, for that it was done by a special spirit, in its kind not imitable by us.

This act of the Lord Jesus being carried on with an eminent and remarkable zeal and magnanimity, gave the disciples an occasion of calling this to mind, "The zeal of thy house hath eaten me up." Of his zeal we have a remarkable discovery in these particulars.

Part 1: The Text Opened

1. In the weakness of the means by which he did both attempt and effect the work; in that the persons but few in comparison, and those despicable in the eyes of the world, Christ and his disciples, not armed with any weapons that might carry dread and terror with them, at most but with a whip made of a few small cords. Which, this kind of whip probably was scattered by the drovers which came there to sell their cattle. And also, to some of them, Christ used only his voice, verse 16, he said to the money changers, "Take these things hence," and it was done.

2. In the strength that the opposite power did hold out, which makes the encounter so much the more dangerous. As first, a garrison of soldiers in *Arce Antonia* were ready at hand to appease (as it is probable) occasional tumults. Secondly, the temper of the men's spirits with whom the business was, for they were men set on gain, the world's *god.* Thirdly, the great confluence of the people, it being the most solemn market of the Passover. Behold then the greatness of Christ's zeal, when neither the weakness of the means on the one side to effect it, nor the greatness of the power on the other side to hinder it, did at all dismay him, or cause him to desist from this attempt of reforming that

so apparent an abuse of the Temple, the house of God. We learn from here, *that:*

Observation: it really does not matter how weak the means of church-reformation is, or how strong the opposite power is, if we can but draw Christ into the business, (Heb. 5:2; Isa. 26:12, 30:21; John 16:13; Jer. 15:20), if we can procure him to sit as President in the Assembly. If he is there, he will heal our ignorances, he will clear up all our doubts, he will guide us by the Spirit of truth, he will be as a wall of brass against all our adversaries, and he will work all our works for us.

I do ingenuously confess, that when we do consider and view the difficulty of the work of church reformation, and our weakness, who are summoned to be advisers in the work, it may amaze us. But when we look on the Lord Almighty, the great Jehovah, the Lion of the Tribe of Judah, to whom nothing is too hard, who has broken through gates of iron, and bars of brass, which we could never have dreamed that they had been penetrated, this again may raise up our spirits, and give us hope, that if we seek the Lord in his way, he will certainly be found of us. "Not by might, nor by power, but by my spirit, saith the LORD of hosts," (Zech. 4:6). It is all one to him, whether by an army and by power, or by quickening the spirits of his, raising them above themselves. Verse 10, "For who hath despised the day of small things?" (Zech. 4:10). Whether by a day of small things, or by doing terrible things that we did not look for, Isaiah 64:3, he brings about his church's cause.[8] It is nothing to him to make mountains plain. "Who art thou O great mountain?" The Lord by the Prophet speaks in a holy scorn of all the enemies the Jews had in rebuilding the temple and city. We accordingly, by a grant from the Right Honorable the two Houses of Parliament, with so many of them as have been pleased to embody themselves with us, are assembled this day to afflict our souls in fasting and prayer before the Lord, that we may seek of him a right way in these great and important affairs to be treated on, that he would give us such a frame of spirit, such an assistance from on high, such a clear light, as may raise us above ourselves. That he may fit us for that work to which we have no sufficiency as from ourselves, (Isa. 8:21). In this way this is how Ezra and the Jews thought about being conscience of their own inability to help themselves in their passage from Babylon to Jerusalem. So we, being now on a further

---

[8] "Who art thou, O great mountain? before Zerubbabel thou shalt become a plain: and he shall bring forth the headstone thereof with shoutings, crying, Grace, grace unto it," (Zech. 4:7).

progress, not from Babylon (as some have unjustly slandered us) but from the remnants of Babylon to the new Jerusalem, our work is (the Lord assisting) to humble our souls before him in a more than ordinary way. O! that the Lord would put us into such a posture of abasement as might make both our persons and services acceptable before him, so should we not doubt but the Lord Christ would be in the midst among us.

The words read to you in John 2, which the disciples remembered, are for the latter part taken out of Psalm 69, uttered by David as a type of Christ, as appears by this application of them. Consider in the verse, first, the Scripture alleged. Secondly, the means by which it came to be alleged. For the latter, it was an act of a sanctified memory in the disciples calling to mind what was written, to which the fact done did serve as a remembrancer. Observe:

Observation: that conscionable reading of holy Scriptures shall be attended with seasonable remembering. That is conscionable reading, when we take up reading the Scriptures in the several seasons which the Lord commands as an act of obedience to him, this shall have seasonable remembering; for so is the promise of Christ, John 14:26, "The Comforter shall bring all things to your remembrance."

How industrious then should we all be in frequent search of Scriptures? Are not they the Paradise of God, in which grows the tree of life, and the leaves are good to heal the nations?[9] Are not Scriptures as that pool to which God has promised a virtual power, in which we may wash and be clean? Scriptures are that golden mine in which we may dig riches that may make us rich to God, that enrich us to eternal life, (as Luther said in his commentary on Genesis 19). So zealous was Luther to have the Scriptures read, that he professed, that if he thought that the reading of his books would hinder the reading of the Scriptures, he would burn them all before he died. But so much of these things briefly; the Scripture itself alleged being that which I intend principally (by God's help) to insist upon. And in this Scripture alleged in the text, three particulars offer themselves. 1. The grace, zeal. 2. The object about which it was conversant, that is God's House. 3. The degree in which it seized on David and Christ, *they were eaten up with it.*

---

[9] Ambrose, Ep. 42.

PART 2: Defining Zeal

Question: First, then, for the grace itself, *What is zeal?* Answer: It is a holy ardor kindled by the Holy Spirit of God in the affections, improving a man to the utmost for God's glory, and the church's good.[10] It is not so much any one affection, as the intended degree of all. Affections are the motions of the will, as carried out to the prosecution of good, or avoiding of evil. They are, as the philosopher speaks, *exitus animae*, the out-goings of the soul. What the wheels are to the cart, the sinews to the body, wings to the bird, the wind to the sails spread, such are the affections to the soul. It is implanted by God to carry the soul here and there as the objects do more or less affect. Man lies like a log, the soul does not move, but it only moves as the affections stir.

For their order they are so placed in the soul, as that they are subservient one to another; they easily provoke the longing appetite. When desiring faculties flag and grow remise by intervenient impediments, then comes in the provoking faculties, as *removens*

---

[10] Zelus est intensus gradus purae affectionis.

impedimenta, as taking away the impediments; and is not this that which is properly called anger?[11]

The second thing is the object, God's *house*. The house of God under the Law, was all the external pledges of God's presence, the altars, temple, tabernacle, ark, *etc.* The house of God under the Gospel, is (as the people of God elsewhere) the ordinances of God here.

The third thing is the degree, "hath eaten me up;" a metaphor taken from men that receive nourishment, and the meat after its several concoctions, is assimilated into the nature of them that receive it. Zeal totally surprises us in what concerns God, so that we mind the things of God, as if we minded nothing else. What was said of Peter, that he was a man made *all of fire?* And of Paul in respect of his sufferings, that he was a "spark of fire burning in the middle of the sea," *Flamma inextinguibilis in medio mari.* This may be much more said of Christ when he was on the work of church reformation.

---

[11] This made Luther to say, *Ira suo loco est optimum Dei donum.*

PART 3: The Doctrine

The text in this way opened, this proposition offers itself. **DOCTRINE:** That church reformation calls for utmost zeal. Our love to promote that work must be such, Song of Songs 4:12, as many waters cannot quench. Our desires must be enlarged, (Psa. 119:20) as those which break through all impediments, admit of no denial, as if we were to say "give me my request or I die," (verse 171). Our hope must be more longing, our endeavors full of activity, our hatred of the opposites more perfect, and our anger in removing the hindrances more violent.

These stirrings of the Spirit expel lukewarmness, induce zeal. Zeal sets on work the whole tide of our affections. Psa. 87:7, "All my springs are in thee," in promoting the good of God's church, David had a spring-tide of his affections, and they all ran in that channel. To what dangers, hazards, and censures did Christ here in the exercise of his zeal expose himself in the case of church reformation! David's zeal for the settling of the ark, how did it make him deny himself in his most necessary refreshings, "I will not go into my house," *etc.* (Psa. 132:3). His house was no house, his bed no bed, his rest no rest; so in his worldly credit, I will yet, for my God's sake, (2 Sam. 6:22), be more vile. So he was in those innumerable heaps of gold and silver, (1 Chron. 29:3) which out of his earnest zeal he had prepared and set apart for the building of the Temple. Nehemiah, that emblem of reformers, what a measure of zeal did he discover in leaving all his court preferments, putting himself in his own person on a risky and tedious journey, in the encounters and oppositions both open and secret. These he met with, in his expensefulness and that to prodigality, as it may seem, for the common cause, in his unwearied persisting in the work until it was accomplished. How iron-like was the spirit of Elijah? How did he, out of a spirit of zeal against the idolatry of Baal, set his face against Ahab, Jezebel, and all the priests of Baal? How was he driven to fly for his life? (Some geographers compute his journey at many hundreds of miles.) How great were the exigences he was put to, even near famishment, to a weariness of his life. John the Baptist, of what an invincible spirit he was. His encounter with a generation of vipers, his bold and daring (for it cost him his life) reproof of Herod for his Herodias, his turning of mountains into valleys, his making of rough ways plain, do all witness to this fact.

The lack of zeal in the people in Jehoshaphat's time, 2 Chron. 20:33, they having "not prepared their hearts to seek the God of their fathers," kept up the high places (2 Chron. 29:36, 30:1) but in Hezekiah's time the zeal of the people plucked them down; the work was done suddenly, for the people were ready. Of such moment it is, that where church reformation is in hand, a spirit of zeal should run in the veins of the Reformers. No such unbecoming evil as, when the cause of God lies at stake, for men to be cold, lukewarm neuters, warping sometimes one way, sometimes another.

PART 4: Zeal in Church Reformation

In the further prosecution of this truth, three particulars do present themselves. 1. Convincing reasons must be rendered, why zeal must be present in church reformation. 2. What influence zeal ought to have in Church-Reformers. 3. How zeal must be qualified, that it may be kept within its bounds; zeal not confined is as wildfire.

For the first of these, three *reasons* offer themselves as arising from the nature of the work in respect of its 1. Excellency. 2. Difficulty. And, 3. The destructive nature of church-evils, if not reformed.

The excellency of the work I argue three ways. Reason 1: In that the work of church reformation is one of God's special favors, by which the Lord would endear his church to him, (Isa. 1:25). When after the church's sad sufferings, he would do his people a special favor, he tells them that he will "purge away all her dross," (Isa. 54:11-13), and take away all her sin. So when the Lord would express himself in the greatest declarations of his love to his church, verse 13, "Oh thou afflicted and tossed with tempest, I will lay thy stones with fair colors, thy foundations with saphires," *etc.* God will set up his ordinances in a more glorious way; "all thy children shall be taught of the Lord." Accordingly in this latter age of the world, what is the great work for which the church blesses God with the song of Moses, and the song of the Lamb, is it not the victory over the beast, his name, mark, *etc.*, all done by church reformation? Rev. 15:3-4, "Great and marvelous are thy works, Lord God Almighty," *etc.*

2. The excellency of the work is argued jointly from the relations between God and his church, and the office which reformers do. In Song of Songs 4:12, the church is God's garden, which being planted with all variety of flowers is apt to be overgrown with weeds, that not only mar its beauty, but eat out the good herbs. Reformers, their work is to weed the Lord's garden, throw out all those noisome herbs which would have spoiled all the good ones. Verse 13, for the church is the Lord's orchard, in which trees of all kinds, both for fruit and medicine, "grow on the banks thereof." The Master of that orchard is impatient of any such trees that encumber the ground, and after many years bear no fruit. Reformers, their work is to root out the plants that God never planted, (Luke 3:6). The church is God's house, where he delights to dwell; reformers are to cast out all

the dirt, dross and garbage that is odious and irksome to the Master of the house. They sweep down all the cobwebs in which the spiders built their webs. The church is God's spouse, (Song of Songs 4:12), in whose "beauty his soul delights." And that she should be deformed with strange attire, ornaments borrowed from notorious strumpets, the Lord cannot endure. Reformers strip her of all her harlotry attire, take off all her Jezebel-like paintings, and render her to Christ in her native simplicity. The church is the Lord's vineyard, (Song of Songs 8:12), which he keeps and waters every moment. Reformer's work is to take out the foxes that destroy the vines. How welcome should the feet of such be? Song of Songs 2:15, and how should the precious nature of the work in relation to God, draw out all our strength?

3. That the excellency of the work may be yet further evidenced: consider it in the objects whereabout it is conversant; that is, either things, or people. Things are doctrine, worship and government. Doctrine is a ray or beam of supernatural truth issued out from God as a special favor to his people, tending to inform them in right notions and apprehensions concerning God, Christ, our souls, and the whole way of salvation. This is

called the word of life, the wholesome word, the word of salvation, etc. How useful is this word, (2 Peter 2:1) since men do as surely perish by damnable heresies, as by moral vices? Doctrine is as the waters of the sanctuary, how great a sin to puddle or poison these! Was it not a capital crime among the Romans to poison the common springs? How noisome was that plague to the Egyptians to have all their waters of which they should drink, turned into blood? Was it not much more (as the soul is more excellent then the body) pestilential to have all the main articles of our religion (not that of justification excepted) to be all, or the most, desperately corrupted, as may be seen in the Ministers Remonstrance exhibited, together with their Petition for Reformation.[12]

  The second particular, about which Reformation is conversant, is worship; by which God and we have communion one with another, and we do in a holy manner trade with God and he with us. This is as Jacob's ladder, the "angels of God ascend and descend by it;" our prayers ascend, God's blessings descend. The ordinances are those golden pipes by which the golden oil empties itself into the hearts of God's people. They are the

---

[12] *Petition* with Remonstrance, exhibited in *Parl.* in January, 1640.

church's breasts from where her children suck nourishment. They are the church's barn and her wine press. They are on Christ's part, the kisses of his mouth, the mutual embraces between God and the Christian soul. Dry up all the breasts in such a city as this, how great will the cry of the infants be? This mischief, by the putting down of preaching, and strange innovations brought and urged on us in our most solemn worship, had in a great part seized on us, and will yet certainly prevail if the Reformers do not seasonably and strongly oppose them.

The third particular is church discipline or government. All societies, and so the church, is upheld by ruling and being ruled. This among other benefits it will yield. That it will preserve the honor of God's censures and ordinances, that great censure of excommunication, which is no less than the delivering up of a man to Satan, and (next to the day of judgement) it is *judicium maxime tremendum*. It shall no longer lackey up and down for duties and fees as it has done among us, and as it did in the darkest times of Popery as Gerson complains.[13] This once established, will direct us

---

[13] Gers. lib *de defectib. Ecclesiasticis*. Quid est qued, etc. Ezek. 22:26. Lib. *de Eccles. defect.* Quid est, quod Gladius Ecclesiae,

to put a difference between the holy and the prophane, the clean and the unclean, for a lack of this is where the Lord challenges the priests. Has not this been, and is it not yet in a great part, remaining on us, as one of our land destroying sin? Is this not the promiscuous thrusting in of scandalous and ignorant people on the sacrament of the Lord's Supper, to the horrible profaning of the same, and no power that would here be allowed as legal, no, not for making a stay of such things? Do not misunderstand me, I do not mean that men should be cut short of that latitude which the laws of Christ allow; only let that hedge and mound of discipline be erected, by which holy things may not be indifferently administered, as well to men egregiously prophane, and that after conviction, as to the Lord his holy ones.

Now to consider things of people. These are as all church officers, of which a ground in Scripture, so more specially, the ministers of the word, the dispensers of holy things. These, if good, are the best of men; as, who are one of a thousand, (Job 33:2; 2 Cor. 5:19), when others at the utmost but one of four or five hundred. To these God has committed the *ministry of reconciliation*

---

scilicet Excommunicatio, extrahitur pro re nihili, ut pro re nummarino?

even of God with men. These the Lord has trusted with the power of opening and shutting heaven, when the same commission is not given to the angels themselves. To which of the angels did God ever say, "Whatsoever ye bind on earth is bound in heaven," *etc.* These are worthily described as a type of savior, "Whose soever sins ye remit, they are remitted unto them; and whose soever sins ye retain, they are retained," (John 20:23). "And saviours shall come up on mount Zion to judge the mount of Esau; and the kingdom shall be the LORD'S," (Obad. 1:21). And of such as these, Reformers hold out a hope; all their endeavors are and ought to be, that the churches, those who have sat in darkness and in the shadow of death, may be furnished with bright shining lights. Now, as these who attend at the altar, if good, they are the best, but if evil, they are the worst. It is as among the mariners who see the wonders of the Lord in the deep, they either are the best or worst of men; the best, if what they see, works for the best; or the worst, if they are not bettered. So, we minister's, whom God acquaints with the depths of Scripture, come off from that privilege either as most prophane, or most holy. "If salt hath lost its savor, what is it good for, but to be cast to the dunghill." What hope of salvation for such, where remedies are turned into loathing and poison.[14] And does not that work, which will in this way reserve all honor to God's ordinances, keep them from the prophane ones, furnish the church with faithful watchmen, and rid us of such burdens as are of all other most insufferable, require our utmost zeal?

Reason 2: The second particular, evincing the necessity of zeal, is the difficulty of the work in respect of the mountainous oppositions which Reformers shall and must encounter with; as first, not only a large-spread, but also an unanimous combination of the churches enemies, Gebal, Ammon and Amaleck, the Philistines and them that dwell at Tyre, and they have consulted together with one consent, *etc.* Pope, Spaniard, French, and the whole generation of the English-Jesuits, Papists, and Prelatical Faction, and Libertines, all looking on the work of Reformation, not only as hindering their design, their good work in hand as they call it, but undermining their kingdom. How industriously vigilant are they in laying out themselves, their heads, hands and purses? They leave no stone

---

[14] Qualis spes salutis esse poterit ubi quae suerint remedia convertuntur in nauseam & venenum, Gerson tract. *de vita,* Cler. Gerson. And hence is that of Chrysostom. 40 in Matthew, Qui unquam vidit Clericum cito respiscentem. Chrysostom. Who ever saw a clergy man easily brought to repentance?

unremoved, that may hinder our work or promote their own. Does not all this challenge our utmost zeal?

Secondly, in respect of the prevailing nature, the close adhering of church-men's (as they are called) sin, with whom Reformers must contest. These are sensuality, ambition, and idleness. It was the monk's bellies, and the cardinal's caps, which (as Erasmus observed) created Luther's greatest trouble. Sensuality is a sin wherever it seizes *maximae adherentiae*, of the greatest adherence, as the school speaks. "For the drunkard and the glutton shall come to poverty: and drowsiness shall clothe a man with rags," (Prov. 23:21). Even though I am smitten, the drunkard says, I will seek it yet again. And of sensual sin it is said, "None that go unto her return again, neither take they hold of the paths of life," (Prov. 2:19). The Philosopher could say, the intemperate man is seldom a penitent man. The guise of such church-men are those which did turn their *scribere* into *bibere*, and their *codices* into *calices*.[15] Such the prophet describes in Isaiah 55:12, "Come, say they, and we will fill ourselves with wine, and tomorrow shall be as today." Another describes them[16] as *patinis magis*

---

[15] Petr. *Blessensis*, Ep. 7.
[16] Fran. Duarerus *de Beneficiis*.

quam paginis incumbents, such belly-gods, which another says of them,[17] no dainties suffice them; as if to be judged rather by their complexion then their profession. Against such evil beasts and slow-bellies, not only the councils and synods, but even Julian himself shall rise up in judgment.[18] Julian perceived that the Christian faith grew and increased by the sobriety and abstemiousness of their ministers, which gave command to his *Arch-Flamine Arsatius,* that his priests should not drink in a tavern. If any should do so he should be removed from his priest's dignity.

And what is to say for that horse-leach wickedness of *ambition,* which has so eaten up the vitals of our clergy-masters, may we not see a picture of them in Balaam, who that he might have been capable of Balack's great preferments, how does he wind and turn himself every way that he might curse God's people, (Num. 22 and 23). How lively does Bernard decipher them, *Curritur in Ecclesiastica, etc.* learned and unlearned run, as if men were to live without all care when they came to a charge.[19] The same author tartly

---

[17] Bernard Serm. 30.
[18] Ancient Concil. Laodic can 24. Concil Carthag. tertium. Synod. Turonensis.
[19] Ad curas Ecclesiasticas ac si sine cura victuri cum jam ad curam pervenerint.

derides them when he speaks on this manner, that they hasten to multiply prebends, from there fly to an Archdeaconry, at length climb up to a Bishopric, and they are not satisfied with that, and yet they believe this is the way to heaven? What such miserable men! So, a forenamed author who lived in the twelfth century,[20] said, by right and wrong, unhappy men, who run to the pastoral chair and do not observe that it is to them a chair of pestilence.

As for the idleness of men in the ministry, may we not justly take up the complaint of the Prophet, "They have eaten the fat," (Ezekiel 34:3), "clothed themselves with the wool, but they have not fed the Lord his flock." May we not speak in the same manner as that "Canon" of Christ-Church, in the beginning of Queen Elizabeth's reign, when men were very backward in preaching. They spoke by a *prosopopeia* to the pulpit itself, "Oh good pulpit how have you offended the Canons of Christ-Church, if you were an ambling palfrey, they would ride on you, if a table well furnished, they would feed on you, if a bed of down, they would sleep on you, if a goodly garment, they would wear you, alas good pulpit, what have you done that none of them

---

[20] Peter. *Blessensis*, Ep. 13.

will preach in you!" Might we not compare well various of our clergy-men to Lepidus in the Orator,[21] who when he lay tumbling in the green grass, cried out, "I wish this is what is meant to labor." This is the sickness of many of them, who when they swagger, haunt taverns, play the Epicures, even then they say, "I wish this is what It meant to feed the Lord's flock." We see how there is a need for men to be made zealous with all of zeal, for they encounter men like this who have these vices deeply seized.

  The third particular that places a difficulty on the work of this present Reformation above the former, is that Reformers have had to deal with the gross thick cloud of Popery, the duncery of the monks and friars, with such palpable corruptions, as many of them were discernable by a common light. But now the work lies with men, many of whom retain the same fundamentals with us, and they have come out of Babylon in respect of its foggy part, yet retain many of its dreg which may in time prove pernicious and help to carry us back again into Egypt. These, many of them, are learned Gamaliels, men renowned for worth and parts, whom for my own part, I love and honor; but yet in such things in which

---

[21] Tull 2. de Orat.

Part 4: Zeal in Church Reformation

God has hidden from them what he has revealed to others, I say, as once Augustine said of his friend, "It is possible that the Lord has revealed greater things to them, given them a clearer light in many of the greatest mysteries of religion." Here is the zeal of Reformers, that they refuse to swallow anything that is unsound, because it is offered as countenanced with authority of men famous for their learning and esteem in the churches. Zeal knows no respect of persons in doing her work.

The fourth particular that makes the work difficult, is Demetrius and his whole train that follow him, who cry out, "Sirs, you know that by this craft we have gotten our wealth," I mean our Chancellors, Commissaries, Officials, Registers, Proctors, and these, what mighty piles of wealth, what large and rich estates have they heaped together! These have been as those canker-worms and caterpillars, who have eaten up almost all the green things of the land. They have formerly picked our purses, scratched our faces, vexed our spirits, hurried us from court to court, and all this has been practiced under a pretense of Reformation. But what have they indeed done by all their specious visitations, have they been any other to us then like the jugler's feast, who on a time invited his friends to a solemn banquet, where they came in great expectation to have their bellies filled. They looked for a table richly furnished with all varieties of cakes. They all set about it. But when they put forth their hands, they brought back nothing but air, rose and departed as hungry as they came; so it has been with us in our most solemn visitations. Or may we as Gerson[22] did sometimes compare the visitors of this kind to the cat, which being by the good housewife, put in the dairy-house to save the cheese from the mice and rats, does more harm then all of them. Yes, where the greatest pretense of good was held out, what have all our visitors and Reformers done more than the Pope's cardinals, whom he sent out in Luther's time to blind the world with a pretense of Reformation? As they, so ours, may well be compared to the fox's tail which raises the dust, but carries none of it away.

The fifth difficulty is a potent army of nonresidents, whose glory has been a polygamy of benefices. An evil which we may well wonder at, that Gospel light being so far advanced as it is, learned and modest men should not be ashamed of it. When, as the

---

[22] Gerson in *Serm. habit.* in Conc. Rhemens.

most learned Divines in the Council of Trent did generally protest against it, as appears by their several tracts.[23] I might urge these men with variety of Scriptures, with arguments of divers kinds; but I refer the Reader to Caranza in his *Tractate de non residentia*, who speaks so fully in this argument, as if his book were translated into English, he would be deemed a Puritan that wrote it. I will only use one argument, which I in this way propound. Every command of a duty necessarily implies all the necessary ways and means by which the duty is to be effected, else the Lord should contradict himself, if he should command a duty and dispense with that without which it cannot be performed. But residence in or near the place where the duty is to be done, is evident by the light of nature.

Whoever asked the question, whether the porter, to whom the care of opening and shutting the door is committed, should reside at the door? Or whether he that governs the ship should sit at the helm? Or whether watchmen are not to attend on the tower over which they are set as watchmen? This is

---

[23] Earth. Caranza. Dom. á Soto Card. Cajetan. *Fran. Torrensis ac.* Naclantus vide Biblioth. Colleg. Eman. ubi tractatus bi amnes in unum volumen compinguntur.

Bellarmine's own argument,[24] which on occasion he makes use of. And where men are apt to plead the discharge of their duty ordinarily by another, the unlawfulness of this I in this way give you great evidence.

1. For that the Lord himself quarrels not only with such deputies as were uncircumcised in heart, for that is but an aggravation; but with deputies *as* deputies. "You have set others to take the charge of my Sanctuary, (Ezek. 44:8), "and have not your selves kept the charge of my holy things." So do our non-residents lay the ark, as Uzza and his fellows did on the cart, when they should have carried it on their shoulders.

2. If deputies would ordinarily serve the turn, why then does the Apostle cry out, 2 Cor. 2:16, "Who is sufficient for these things?"

3. Such as are chosen to the work of the ministry, are chosen for their special gifts, not that they can chose others.[25]

4. No man to whom a trust, with respect to his fidelity is committed, may devolve his trust to another, unless it is expressed that way in his contract; it is a

---

[24] Bellarm. in *Ep. ad Nepot.*
[25] Electa est industria tua, non alterius, Caranza.

ruled case among the civilians. But there is no such liberty granted by Christ in that way.

5. Why should Christ admit of that in those to whom he commends the care of souls, that no master of a family will admit in any of his servants, that when he has hired them at such a rate to do his work, they shall ordinarily serve him by those whom they hire at a lower rate?

But may it not make non-residents blush (if they have so much modesty as my hope is some have) if they look on it, first, in its origin. Secondly, in the indirect shifts by which it was upheld in the Council of Trent. Thirdly, in the expressions concerning it, as they have been uttered by friars, cardinals, and popes themselves. For its origin[26] among many other grounds not now to be insisted on. Was it not at first brought in to maintain the Pope's magnificence, who having gotten large territories to himself, when he would advance himself above all the Western monarchs, saw it necessary (that he might not be as an owl among the birds) to make great his cardinals by a worldly pomp. This that he might effect, he challenges to himself, as the privilege of

---

[26] Conc. Trid. lib. 2. Bucer de vi & usu Sacr. Minist. Franc. Duaren. de benef. l. 5. C. 7.

Peter, the collation of all Ecclesiastical Dignities. And he does it to the end that he might enrich his cardinals, and make them princes and fellows. He gave dispensations to several men to hold.[27] This made a great accession to his greatness, when those of his conclave were able to maintain such a state.

Secondly, for the carriage of the cause in the Council of Trent, we must know, that the several Popes who lived in the time of the Council, gave it a special charge to their legates. That among other things to be reformed in the Court of Rome, they should be sure that non-residence should suffer no damage. And accordingly, when that business came in question, the legates found out a diversion at least six several times. And in the issue, when the Spanish Divines pressed the cause so far, as it could not be avoided, but a Canon must be made against it, the pope creates forty titular bishops,[28] sends them to the Council, and by that means was the cause carried so that though a Canon was made against it, yet with such *provisos*, as makes it to be of no effect.

---

[27] Nic. Clemang. *de corrup.* fla. Eccles. ducenta, trecenta, quadringinta, & quinginta Beneficia etc.
[28] Gentiletus in *Exam*, Conc, Trid. l. 4. f. 23.

Part 4: Zeal in Church Reformation

Thirdly, for the expressions of the Popish party, one says, "Since Christ's ascension, there is no greater evil in the church then a plurality of benefices."[29] Another says, "That but that it is supposed they have the church's absolution at their death, they ought not to have the benefit of Christian burial." Another calls the distinction of residence and non-residence, a distinction never enough to be detested. Another says, that anciently men were admonished to be a resident, but it never came under dispute. One of the former counts the justification of this evil to be a choking of the light of nature, a shutting of our eyes in it. We read of two popes, Clement the fifth, and Vide Francis. Gregory the eleventh, who being visited by the hand of God, did, out of the sense of their sin, make void all their dispensations for non-residents. What a measure of zeal is required to reform them, whom all this does not shame!

The sixth difficulty that will exercise a Reformers zeal, is the multitude adhering to their old customs, idolizing their formalities. We may see the genius of the people in this regard in those of Jer. 44, "What thou hast spoken to us in the name of the Lord we will not do, but we will do so and so." And in Judges

---

[29] Cajetan. in tract. de non-resident.

18:24, Micah, who when the Danites had taken away his idols, he goes after them with hue and cry; they demanding, what ails the man? He makes this reply, "Have you taken away my gods, and do you ask me what I ail?" You see the prevalence of old customs in the people called Hircani, who when their King went about to alter a heathenish custom of casting their dead to mastiff dogs instead of burial, he had likely to have lost both his life and crown. This impatience of the people to have anything altered, the papists will shame us; for who in the times of Paulus tertius, and Pius quintus, though they professed infallibility in their way, yet have they yielded to have their breviaries twice changed.

And in this way, you have the second reason, why zeal is of great use.

Reason 3: A third convincing reason of the necessity of zeal, is, the destructive nature of those evils, which if Reformation does not remove, will be the ruin of Kingdoms. Consider the wickedness of ministers. When the Lord calls for all the beasts of the field to devour and spoil Jerusalem, the sore-runner of this was the wickedness and idleness of the priests, Jer. 23:15, "Doth not wickedness go from them into all the land?" "Thy watchmen are blind," (Isaiah 56:10-11), they are all dumb dogs, they cannot bark. They are greedy dogs, (Lam. 2:15), they all look to their own way, everyone is out for his gain from his quarter. So, when Jeremiah mentions the cause of Jerusalem's destruction, he inserts this, "Thy Prophets have looked out for the vain and foolish things. They have not discovered thine iniquity, to turn away thy captivity," *etc.* So in the tenth century,[30] which was most barren of all good writers, and fruitful in all manner of wickedness, in which the Pope got up on horseback, what did a good writer of the clergy of that time, say, "What do we ministers who are so much the more inferior to others in holiness of life, as we are more eloquent in words, who stirring up others fall asleep ourselves, holding out light to others, are so much the more darkened in ourselves."[31] So when Antichristianism and Islam grew to their full maturity,[32] was it not then when the prelates became *idol* shepherds, when the pastors became wolves, and the angels of the churches, devils? Was not the wickedness of the priests a principal in-let of the Saxons to expel the Brittains out of this land? A good author said, they have

---

[30] Vide Cent. 10. Magdeburg
[31] Ansb. in Apoc. lib. 5. c. 11.
[32] An. Dom. 1300. Hug. in Psa. 104.

priests, but foolish ones, they do not understand.[33] These pastors, as they are called, but indeed wolves, ready to slay the souls of the people, not seeking the good of the people, but the fulness of their own bellies *etc.* So, for matter of doctrine, when the Saxons invaded this land, the Pelagian heresy had with a filthy contagion defiled the Brittain's faith.[34] Should not zeal stir itself, when such evils as these overspread a state?

---

[33] Brittany, Vide Gild. a p. 58. ad finem.
[34] Beda lib. 1. c. 7.

PART 5: Zeal in Reformers

The second head to be considered, is what influence zeal ought to have *into* Reformers.

First, zeal will and must do her work thoroughly. It is God's work. Men must not work it in halves. There is a danger that the least corruptions grow again, unless they are pulled up by the roots. Experience has taught what sad persecutions a partial reformation has made way for. What hope does such an imperfect proceeding give to the enemies, that we will come on to them again.

Secondly, Zeal must and will summon all the powers of soul and body, and all that we can prevail with, to further the work. God delights in men of activity, he does not care for the *dull ass* to be offered in sacrifice, for its neck was to be broken. It was earnest Baruch that had the praise above the rest.[35] The twelve Tribes *served* God. What should we be earnest for, if not for God and his cause? Will you be earnest for your friend, your profit, your pleasures, and cold for your God?

---

[35] "After him Baruch the son of Zabbai earnestly repaired the other piece, from the turning of the wall unto the door of the house of Eliashib the high priest," (Neh. 3:20).

Thirdly, after zeal is convinced of the justice of the cause, over-looks all dangers though never so great. So, Caleb, when he heard of the difficulties, resolves, "Let us go up at once." So, Esther said, "If I perish, I perish." So, Paul said, "What do thee, weeping and breaking my heart?" It also treads under foot all allurements, all hope of great things. God now as good as says, "That which I have planted," (Jer. 45:4-5), "I will pluck up, and seekest thou great things for thyself?" Is it now a time to receive money, and to receive garments, and olive yards, and vineyards, and sheep and oxen?

Fourthly, zeal helps a Reformer against the temptation of being alone. This prevails much, especially where the devil and our carnal friends seek out an advantage against us, and amplify the discouragement. How have the mighty been here overthrown? Zeal takes notice, for the support of herself. Consider Joshua's resolution, "Choose ye whom ye will, but I and my house will serve the Lord," (Joshua 24:15). So, of Elijah's complaint, that he was left alone, (1 Kings 19:10). So, of Paul in 2 Timothy 4, "At my first answering no man assisted me." Zeal takes notice that numbers begin in one, and had there not been one first, there had never been two.

Part 5: Zeal in Reformers

Fifthly, zeal commands perseverance, and holding out in the work. Many begin in the spirit, but end in the flesh. How many brave worthies that blossomed fair, come on as promising great things, yet have split them on the rock of an unfound heart, withered away, if not in the end proved false to God and their country. They might have been worthy patriots for a time, but their hearts failing them, they prove to be such as relinquish their station. *Christianis non initia sed fines laudantur;* "he only receives the crown that overcomes." That heat in a Reformer that is from heaven will hold out, not that which is merely advantageous, set on work from outward causes.

PART 6: How Zeal Must Be Qualified

The third head takes up the question as to how zeal must be qualified.

1. It must be founded in knowledge. The understanding is the eye of the soul. As metal is dangerous in a blind horse, so zeal is like this when it is not directed by a judgment which is well informed. Zeal, as fire, must have light as well as heat. It is hell where there is heat and no light but utter darkness.

Like the mind, so zeal cannot be good without knowledge. The Jew's zeal, was defective in that it was "not according to knowledge," (Romans 10:2). This zeal must not be conjectural, probably seeming, such only as we have received from others without examination. There is nothing more ordinary then plentiful allegations of Scripture to carry a cause; it does not matter how specious and frequent quotations of Scripture there are, as what they prove on in a sound trial. You whom God has entrusted with this work, do not take everything for gold that glisters.

2. It must be ordered with wisdom. Zeal must be wary, as well as warm. Fire is good, but in a wise man's

hands, that will not put it into the thatch; fire is good in the chimney, but if it catches the rafters of the house it sets everything on fire. In the encounter with sin and wickedness, to be reformed in this, biblical wisdom will have a reformer to set on reforming, *Quando necesse id, ut sit impar vitio,* knowing that will but enrage sin all the more. There are many mischiefs that men will fall into without wisdom, men that mean well are subject to even their good endeavors, (Eccl. 10). But wisdom is profitable to direct one in the right path. Beware here of that over weary discretion that destroys what is real.

3. It must be tempered with love. Zeal is apt to be harsh, but love lines the yoke and makes it easy to be borne. Augustine said "Love takes us off from all bitterness to men's persons. Love and say what you will."[36] Love allows us to be warm, sharp, home in our reproofs, but not scalding hot. The stomach does not admit that which burns the lips, nor the ear that reproof that is contumelious. Love calls on us as to be zealous for the truth, so to make it our work to endeavor to "keep the unity of the Spirit in the bond of peace," (Eph. 4:3). What should rend and divide us one from another, whom the Lord has united with so many bonds, as to

---

[36] August. in *Galat. 6.*

meet in one God, one Christ, one Spirit, one faith, one baptism, one heaven?

Far be it from us, on whom the Apostle has laid so many charges, "if any consolation in Christ," (Phil. 2:1), "if any comfort of love, if any fellowship of the Spirit, if any bowels and mercies fulfill my joy, that ye be of one accord and one mind." Do not our adversaries study to make divisions among us? Shall we gratify them, and weaken ourselves? Do not they cry out that if they can but divide us they shall conquer us? It is memorable what is reported of Julian,[37] that he did nourish dissentions among Christians.

---

[37] Amian. Marcell. *de Julian*, lib. 22.

PART 7: Uses to Reformers

Use 1: If zeal is so requisite a grace in him that God calls to be a Reformer, then we must give diligence that our zeal may be of the right stamp. As every grace so zeal may and often has its counterfeit, *as:*

First, if it lacks a true light. There are false lights that mislead men over bogs and dangerous places; we are exceedingly apt to be misled when prejudiced by men's persons, their learning or holiness, antiquity, or novelty, as if we were necessarily to receive a thing because ancient, or to reject it because it is new, by a hasty engaging of our judgments before we are able to judge, and an unwillingness to retract when we have judged by an undue enquiry. This is when we rather seek that things may be lawful, then whether they are lawful or not. This is when we are transported by self-conceitedness of our own opinion. It is only the eye-salve of the Spirit by the Word which must guide us, "To the Law and to the Testimony," (Isa. 8:20).

Secondly, if it does not suffer itself to be ordered by wisdom. This takes in right means as conducing to a right end. There is a precipitance in zeal by which he that hastens in his matters, sins. There is a spirit of deliberation and counsel; consider, consult, then give sentence, (Eccl. 10:25), then practice. A good cause often miscarries by indiscreet handling. The labor of the foolish man wearies every one of them, because he does not know how to go to the city. Ignorance of the right means, tires out men in their endeavors to no purpose.

Thirdly, if it easily falls into wrangling and quarrels. Love, that is and ought to be the orderer of zeal, "suffereth long," (2 Cor. 13:1ff), and it "beareth all things, endureth all things." Love knows that a little breach will quickly be a great one. It prevents them or speedily makes them up. It gives the water no passage, no not a little. Zeal for God is tenderly respectful of men's persons. When it does not respect a person, it is a wild-fire and not zeal, (Dan 5:15; Acts 26:24). Wildfires cast fire-brands and arrows, and deadly words, and says falsely, "I mean no harm," (Prov. 26:18-19).

Fourthly, if zeal is right, she will not be in an angry mood concerning what lies under the command of God, no not a bit. It is false zeal that cries, "neither mine nor thine, but let it be divided," that makes nothing of small matters. True zeal drives on the work of Reformation so as it does not leave the least remnants of Baal, removes all high places, as considering that great persecutions, have been raised on small matters, and that conscience is a tender thing, as the eye, where the least speck troubles it.

Fifthly, if our zeal is only flashy, (like those unnatural heats that come and go by flushings), it is not right. We have many that begin well, are hot and eager while in such a company, while they have such props, while carried on by such hopes, while not assaulted with such-temptations, while they thought the cause would go in this way. Then they were hot and eager in the work of Reformation, but as things alter from without, they alter from within, even to the total remitting of their zeal.

Sixthly, if one has true zeal, as that which has the cause of God in the eye, then any tract of time, multitude of discouragements, falseness of men deserting the cause, strength of oppositions will not tire out a man's spirit. Zeal makes men resolute. Difficulties are but sharpening stones to their fortitude. It makes a man's spirit as if it were made of steel with an undaunted magnanimity.

Use 2: If zeal is so necessary in a Reformer, then we are all first to bless God for that fire of zeal the Lord has kindled in many of your hearts, (right Honorable and beloved) by which you have been willing to spend and to be spent for the common cause. We may read of your zeal in your unwearied pains, in your denial of yourselves in matters of profit and pleasure, in the many hazards you have run, even of all you are, have, or may expect in the railings and speakings of men against you. Have not we cause to be thankful for your zeal by which you have taken off unsufferable burdens from our backs, for the many snares from which you have for the discovery of and delivery of us from most dangerous ruining plots, for the many precious ordinances of Parliament that have issued out for the common good? Have not many unworthy scandalous and soul-starving ministers been displaced, and good ones placed in their room? Has not the Lord's Day been restored to its pristine sanctification, and (by burning the *Book of Sports*, with other commands for better sanctifying the day) been vindicated from all those former unsufferable profanations? How have superstitious monuments been defaced, secret idolatries suppressed, seducers of the people been banished the land. For all these, and many more, everlasting honor shall be on your head as our Reformers. Go on and prosper (you Noble Parliament Worthies) work worthily in our *Ephrata*, and be famous in our *Bethlehem*. So shall the Lord make your names as a savory ointment, crown you with his best blessings, make your families flourish when you are dead and gone, remember you according to all the good you have done for God's cause. But above all, that you have found out a way in these distracted times (in which religion itself, groans under the wantonness of our people, loathing the manna, and hunting after novelties, under the uncouth and irreligious opinions crept in among us, under the bitter divisions that overspread city and country) to call an Assembly of able and Worthy Divines, with whom you might advise for the settling of doctrine, worship, and discipline. (O! that this work had been sooner in hand!) Not only have you found such a way, but you have embodied many worthies from among yourselves with us. Have not we a double benefit by this; first, you by your association, put honor on us who should without you in the eyes of many carnal men have been very despicable. Secondly, by this happy conjunction, you both help to order us who are ignorant of the nature of such meetings, and with by a seasonable interposal may stop divisions among us. Only we have a double suit to you.

1. That you would not suffer the work to be either spun out beyond what is necessary, or yet hastily slobbered over. Not the first, for that the enemy is sowing tares, and much harm may be done while we are consulting. Errors may enter so deeply, that they may prove incurable. Nor yet let it be done negligently. First, for that it is the Lord's work, to its negligent doing belongs a curse. Secondly, Jer. 48:10, in that it is to us of near concern, all our wealth goes in this bottom. Thirdly, for that many eyes are on us from abroad, both of friends who will praise God for what we do well, and of foes who watch for our halting.

2. Our second suit to you is, that when the Laws of Christ, for the due administration of his ordinances, shall be discovered, you would be pleased to account it your greatest honor to submit to them. Christ's government is the only liberty, thralldom to your lusts is the only true bondage. If you honor God, he will honor you. It is his Gospel that has clothed you with scarlet, put ornaments of gold on you, put every precious stone in your garments. Do not be jealous, as if Christ's Government would eclipse your greatness. Christ's rule and your honors are not incompatible. The Lord Jesus tells us his Kingdom is not of this world, he commands

that Caesar have his right. It is the description of the Spirit of God that calls you worthy dignities (with respect to which the school allows that outward pomp which magistracy is honored with) and the same spirit mentions the pomp of Agrippa, when he came to sit in judgement, without dislike, (Acts 25:23).

Secondly, as it sets out the unspeakable good of a zealous Reformer, and what a blessing such a one is, so it points out to us what that is, which of all others is most uncharacteristic of a Reformer, *viz.* the lack of zeal, which will render such whom God has called to this office, most odious to him, most abominable to men. Ages present will count themselves unfortunate in such. Ages to come will curse such opportunities which God afforded them, and which they for lack of zeal have squandered away. These will rise up in judgement against them. What might such have done, if a spirit of zeal had eaten up their spirits? They might have saved the churches at home and abroad, given Antichrist that blow that should have thrown him as a mill-stone into the middle of the sea, delivered liberties, laws, and inheritances to posterity, saved city, country, the lives of millions of men, they might have finished the work they began, all succeeding ages might have blessed God for them, their own works may have praised them in the gate. Now if zeal is lacking, they will undo all the churches of Christ, as much as in them lies. They will uphold tottering Babylon, destroy flourishing England, deliver up their posterity to absolute slavery, make themselves the monuments of shame and ignominy to all that know or shall hear of them. "Oh tell it not in Gath, publish it not in the streets of Askelon," *etc*. Must it not necessarily be so when so necessary a core, fundamental grace as zeal is lacking? For what is a Reformer without zeal, but as a body without a soul, a bee without a sting, a soldier without his weapon, a bird without wings, salt without savor? Oh then you Noble Senators, who are under God the chariots and horse-men of our Israel, whatever you part with, do not part with your zeal, let this be your honor and crown, and as a diadem on your head, that yet you are zealous for your Religion, your country, your laws, and liberties. Shall you but remit your former zeal, a spirit of lukewarmness (which God forbid) seizes on you, and you sell truth for peace. You will live and die without honor if you do this, and render yourselves and us as the most miserable nation under heaven.

Use 3: Let me address myself to you, Right Reverend and beloved in the Lord. Behold the Lord has, by his providence, singled us out among our brethren, for this great work in hand. Both you and we all are desirous this day to lay ourselves low before the Lord, importunately to intreat his assistance, that he would be pleased to magnify his power in our weakness. He might have made a choice of many of our brethren every way as able, if not more able then ourselves, but so is his pleasure, and we do not dare but be at his disposal. The Lord can work as well by the oaten pipe, as by the silver trumpet. Be then exhorted by him who reckons himself the meanest of you all, and who in respect of his many infirmities might well have been dispensed with. Be, I say, exhorted to clothe yourselves, out of respect to the work in hand, with zeal as with a cloak, to fall on the business you are designed to, *toto animi impetu*, you are called out to contend for the truth that was once given to the saints, which has been sealed with the blood of martyrs, has been justified by the learned pens and disputes of all the worthies of this kingdom, without interruption, for above this 80 years. It is but of late pained by a cunning, ambitious, and corrupt party, we had almost been cheated of it, even of that truth which ought to be dearer than our lives.

    Blessed be our God who has given a turn, and made a stop of their proceedings, whose work was, as to put out the eyes of the people of the land by ignorance, so to have leavened them with heterodox opinions, and were we not indeed gone almost as far as Rome's gates in a declining way? Our work is a noble work, it is *servare depositum*, to be trustees for that saving truth, that pattern of wholesome words, which has been derived to us, as from the pure fountain of Scripture. And it has well come to us by the channel of purer antiquity as it comes with *letters of commendation* from the sufferings of God's choicest servants. They were such whom the world was not worthy of. I implore you in the bowels of Jesus Christ, we may quit ourselves like men, do our utmost, that we may vindicate the truth of God from all the aspersions of evil-minded men, clear it from those ambiguities by which ungodly men have perplexed it, and do such further work, in worship and discipline, as shall by God and man be required of us. What would our ancestors, those glorious lights of former times, have given to have had such a price put into their hands, as we unworthy ones at this time have?

May we not justly think, that what opportunity we have, is but the effect of the fervent prayers, the many tears, and sad sufferings of our sage and reverend predecessors, that are now with the Lord? Are there not already on us in this work for which we are assembled, the eyes of our brethren of the Reformed Churches, as expecting the issue of this business? No, is not the whole nation in expectancy of what this meeting will produce? What manner of people ought we to be, in humbling of our souls before the Lord, crying mightily to him who alone keeps the key of the cabinet, unlocks the secrets of his will, opens the eyes of our understandings! (Luke 24). Can we look backward, to the many brave excellent-spirited and well-parted men, who have turned some to Justinian, some to Galen, some to Littleton, others taken themselves to a retired privacy, which long ago might have sat in Moses' chair, had there not stood the fiery blade of corruptions in worship and government to keep them out? How many silver trumpets, that might have made sweet melody in God's house, have been hung on the willow trees, and all because this work was not done? How many hundreds of worthy, learned, soul-saving ministers, men excellently fitted for the work, have been driven out of our land? (May the Lord lay it not to our charge.) It is no small affliction to be put on disserting of one's native country, and all those *charitates* which under God are the life of our life, and further to be cast on foreign countries. They are those sometimes unwholesome for our English bodies, placed among inhumane people, put upon wildernesses, wild beasts, savage people, and unknown necessities, because by reason of our sins this work has not been yet affected, they saw no hope of it. O! the swarms of godly men, that like Noah's dove, could find no rest for the soles of their feet, being hunted up and down, hurried here and there, and wasted with vexatious suits, to their utter undoing, who have been in the end forced, they and their whole families, with heavy hearts, and some with poor estates, to bid farewell to dear England, as never to see it again? These would have been content to have lived in a smoky house, and a mean condition with freedom of conscience. Yes, they have been put on it to commit themselves rather to the merciless rage of the tempestuous seas, to a long, tedious and irksome sea-journey, by which they were utterly unacquainted, rather than to endure those sad impositions which were charged on their consciences. And now the Lord puts it into the hands of you, the right

Honorable, that sit at the stern in point of reformation utterly to remove. What shall I say to those millions of souls, who have perished through the negligence, insufficiency, scandalous and corrupt proceedings of that order of men,[38] which it is to be hoped, if our iniquities do not hinder, will be rectified by that *clericalis disciplina*, which learned Mr. Bucer did so often call for in King Edward VI's days.

To this end I once again do humbly beseech you, men, brethren, and fathers, that you would take up the practice of such holy duties, as may conduce to this so pious, so necessary a work.

1. And first let us all stir up in ourselves the gift of prayer, (2 Tim. 1:6). Let it be frequent, fervent, and full of faith. You know the efficacy of prayer, (Isa. 45:11), it sets God on work, and that with a holy kind of command. It has an omnipotence with it; it never went of any errand and returned empty. Be confident if God does but stir up our hearts in prayer he will come in and help us in the work. What if we are weak? Psa. 10:17, yet he is strong. What if we lack, in our own apprehension, those abilities fit for the work? He can lift us up above ourselves, and supply us with help. What if we lack that

---

[38] Bucer inopus. In tractatu *de vi & usu minisleris*, 191.

quickness of understanding, those activity of parts, we see in others? Yet if we can but assist and encourage others, God will accept it. Only resolve of this, no man was ever a successful reformer without a Spirit of prayer. Elijah and Luther tell us so much. To encourage us, God's promises stand sure, Jer. 33:3, "Ask of me and I will shew the great and hidden things, which thou knowest not." Or, Proverbs 25, "If thou seekest for wisdom as for silver," *etc.*, "if thou cryest after knowledge," *etc.*, then "shalt thou understand the fear of the Lord, the knowledge of God." We do not attain truth only by disputing, but by learning from him who only knows, said one of the Ancients.[39] Luther said, that prayer, reading, meditation and temptation, do complete a divine.

    2. Secondly, that God may impart to us that way of sincerity in his worship, that form of government, which may be most according to his will, (a favor worth the knowing, and which God refuses not to acquaint them with that fear him; Psalm 25, his secret is revealed to such). Let our study be to be *doers* of his will. If the glass is clean, then do not soil the clean water that is poured into it, and if needs be, we pour in more. If

---

[39] Lact. lib. 7 c. 2.

otherwise, we hold our hands. So, the Lord does this with us that are ministers, for he will not pour the sweet water of truth, but into the sanctified heart. "If any man," John 7:27, the Evangelist says, "will do his will, he shall know of the doctrine, whether it be of God or no." There is among the brethren many perplexed disputes, and much difference, whether this is the form Christ has left. These distractions are sadly to be lamented. Would we be able to wind ourselves out of these labyrinths of disputes, see the good and right way God would have us to walk in, take notice of that promise in Ezekiel, Ezek. 43:11, "If the house of Israel shall be ashamed of their iniquities, and of all that they have done, I will shew them the form of the house," *etc.*, then only here we must beware. We do not dare to offer to God's people such a form, as does not have its ground out of plain places of Scripture, but such only as are typical and allegorical. *Allegorica Theologia*, (unless the Lord himself makes the application) *non est argumentative*. It is our error that often times we do *afferre sensum ad Scripturam non referre*. We are oftentimes in imagining forms of government, like that sect of Philosophers, who having drunk in this principle, that all the world was made of numbers, where ever they went, they thought they saw numbers. If the Lord shall but behold us loathing ourselves for our ways that have not been good, disallowing our sins, personal and national, (Luke 24), setting our hearts in a right frame, then will he open our understandings that we may know the Scripture.

Thirdly, that God may so far delight in us, as to make us instruments of such a glorious work as this is, let us take all occasions to dispense the holy truths of God to his people. The more we pour out, the more God will pour in. The oil in the cruse increased by pouring out for the woman tending Elijah; the bread with which Christ fed his followers multiplied in its breaking. It is true that this duty has been looked on of late as that which had neither form nor beauty. Was it not our shame that even Bellarmine,[40] yes, the Council of Trent itself, should describe preaching *Praecipuum Episcopi officium*, the chief duty of a bishop, when we suppressed it, put gags in the mouths of the preachers, cast all scorn on it? The Lord be blessed, who has in a degree restored it to its pristine dignity, opened the mouths that were stopped, encouraged the faithful preachers. O!l that our sins may not make the shadow of the dial to go back! A main danger here may be from those that will thrust in

---

[40] Session 5.

upon this work that are not fit for it, that will be *canales* before they are *conchae*, channels to let out before they are vessels to retain.[41] There is in many an effusion before infusion. Excellently that father said, "We cut not green wood to build with, but we first season it, lest it shrink and deceive us."[42]

Why do we not observe, that such are not to be admitted to the ministry that are novices, (1 Tim. 3:6)? It was the complaint of Basil, that though no man could obtain the name, no not so much as of a painter, but he must first have mingled many colors, yet men are easily found fit for the ministry.[43] As the poets gave a false appearance to the giants, we make them saints one day, and we bid them be wise and learned men another day, which have learned nothing, nor brought anything to the ministry, but only their wishes.

And now my dear brethren, whom I love and honor, give me leave to remember you of the Prophet Ezekiel's sad threatening, and Saint Paul's deep charge. "If the watchman see the sword come, and blow not the Trumpet, and the people be not warned, their blood will I require at the watchman's hands." So stony, so iron

---

[41] Bernard in *Cant. Serm. 18.*
[42] Greg. *Ep. 95.*
[43] Greg. Naz. Orat, in *Laudem.*

hearted a man as whom this Scripture would not amaze. And Erasmus says of these words, they are rather thunderbolts then words, such thunderbolts which the Judge of all the world will dart against negligent pastors. Blood-guilt is a sad sin, but guilt of soul-blood is more dreadful and inexpiable. We may have many sins, but beware we do not add this to all the residue. No such remarkable plague fell ever upon any family, as on that of Eli for the wickedness of Hophni and Phinehas, who made people to abhor the offerings of the Lord, (1 Sam 3). The wickedness of Eli's house shall not be purged with sacrifice or offering forever. As for Saint Paul's deep charge on Timothy, weigh it thoroughly. 2 Tim. 4:1-2, "I charge thee before God and the Lord Jesus Christ, who shall judge the quick and the dead, in that his appearing and in his Kingdom, preach the Word, be instant in season and out of season." At other times it suffices to urge God's name, here the sweet name of the Lord Jesus, that is honey in the mouth, music in the ear, a joyful shout in the heart, is pressed. At other times the name of Jesus Christ suffices. Here he sets it on by an argument taken from the glorious and last appearing of Christ, and that to judge the quick and the dead, which will be a day of terror, and such a day where in Christ will cast it in the teeth of every idle minister.⁴⁴ How heavy an account will that be to those to whom the Lord has said, *occupy your talents until I come*, when the Lord shall call them to a reckoning, and every one come in and say, *Lord here are the souls you hast given me;* and what if you are an idle or scandalous minister, who has built with one hand and destroyed with another, has nothing to offer but a poor lean ignorant starved flock, when others bring in large harvests. How sad will your account be! If terror will not frighten us, then let the glorious crown that abides every faithful minister work on us, for such there is laid up a "crown of righteousness," (2 Tim. 4:8), a crown that does not wither, (1 Peter 5:4). He says to the faithful, "enter into thy Masters joy, thou hast been faithful in a little, I will make thee ruler over many." Shall not they that win many souls to God shine as stars for ever? (Dan. 11:3). Do not all the contents that are apt to bias us from our work, fall short of that eternal weight of glory? Consider that we do not have other ways to go to heaven as other men think they do. Magistrates if they

---

⁴⁴ Perditam non quaesivisti, thou hast not sought the sheepe that was lost, redde rationem villicationis, give an account of thy stewardship. Ibisid est, in die judic it) Petrus cum Iudea, bi Paulus conversum mundum post se ducens apparebit, etc. Ibi omnes dominicae gregu arietescum animarumlucris apparebunt, nos miseri, etc. qui pastores hic vocati sumus & ibi gregem non ducmus, Gregor. *hom. 7.* livan.

rule well, rich men if they distribute liberally and give to the poor, private men by diligence in their calling, but a minister can go no way to heaven but by faithfully attending the Lord's flock. Yes, if it could be so that there should be no reward that abides a zealous faithful teacher (which notwithstanding is surely laid up in heaven) yet the very comfort that arises from the diligent doing of our duties, would abundantly recompence all our pains. Is there any joy, any dance, that can more cheer up a man's spirit, then the comfort of a soul won to Christ?[45] Let other men enjoy their fat and rich preferments, hunt after dignities, be called of men rabbi; as for us, if we can say, here are the children the Lord has given us, it suffices. Let others say, who will give us such a Bishopric, such a Deanery, such a rich parsonage; a good minister will say, as the king of Sodom said to Abraham, "Give me the persons (so many converts) take thou the goods to thyself." Was ever Caesar more glorious in his diadem, when he put down whom he would, and set up whom he pleased, when he rode in triumph before whole Armies of Captives, (Rom. 15:17), then Paul when he glories how he had spread the Gospel from Jerusalem, and all the circumjacent countries to

---

[45] Ecquod gaudium, Erasmus *Ecclesiast.* ecquod tripudium, etc.

Part 7: Uses to Reformers

Illyricum? "I have whereof, I may glory through Jesus," *etc.*

And on the contrary, is there any such wounding cross, is there any such torturing fury that can so torment and eat up the heart, as when an unfaithful Minister shall seriously and in cold blood weigh what heaps of souls he has been a means to plunge forever into the infernal lake? Can his bravery, his luxury, his good companions, his jollity? Can the excellency of his parts and learning, his applause in the world privilege him, when the hand writing shall appear on the wall? Surely when a minister shall lie upon his deathbed, nothing can uphold his drooping spirit, but the testimony of his conscience, that he has "fought a good fight, kept the faith." This alone must be our Paradise.

Finally, my Brethren, consider that God has engraved our duties on our names? We are watchmen, shepherds, workmen, builders, the Lord's husbandmen, his soldiers, if we slack or forget our duties, we shall forget our names. No, our names will be our accusers; the ground of the Lord's quarrel against us. That which of old was given in charge to a Roman Consul,[46] the same

---

[46] Pium nomen est reatus impii, Salv. *de provid.,* lib. 4. Consul es praesta nomen.

should every one of us enforce on ourselves, "See to it that you minister and shepherd for you will provide me with you your name." I conclude with that of Jerome, "Read what your name is, and be what you are called."[47]

---

[47] In Ep. ad Nepot.

PART 8: The Best Way to be Zealous in Preaching

And now, beloved, having endeavored to quicken you and myself to the duty of preaching, give me leave to suggest something concerning the manner that it may be done to the best purpose. The Lord requires not only that we preach the Word, but so to preach it as that our hearers may be brought on to the faith. Acts 14:1, Paul and Barnabas are said so to have taught that multitudes believed. If it is an advantage to a hearer in his work how he hears, is it not so to a preacher how he preaches? That our ministry may be *successful:*

1. First, we must preach zealously; that was the honor of John the Baptist, that he was a burning light, (John 5:35). It was of Saint Paul, that with respect to the idolatry at Athens, his spirit was stirred within him (Acts 17); so, of Apollos it is witnessed, that he was fervent in spirit, (Acts 18:25). This zeal must show itself by a holy indignation against sin. It is reported of Saint Chrysostom,[48] that he reproved sin against God, as if he himself had received an injury. It appears also by enlarged desires, that the souls of the hearers may be

---

[48] Sozemen. lib. 8. c. 2.

brought to God. So, in Paul, (Rom. 9:3), "I could wish myself accursed from Christ," *etc.* This zeal in a preacher will put life and quickness into their expressions. Men of cold and dead spirits, their words die in their mouths, and usually beget a coldness in their hearers. Zeal is as resin to the strings of the musical instrument, without which it makes no sound. Only, as the good as the fire on the hearth is enlarged or lessened according as the family occasions, so according to the nature of the offences, as great or small, should the preacher's zeal be proportioned.

2. Secondly, we must preach compassionately; what else is insinuated in those phrases, in which God is brought in, speaking as putting on the bowels of a man, (Deut. 5:25; Ezek. 33:11) and teaching us to do so. It is said of Christ, that he had compassion on the people, for that they were as sheep without a shepherd, (Matt. 9:36), and in another place speaking to Jerusalem, how compassionately does he express himself, "O Jerusalem, Jerusalem," (Matt. 23:37), "how would I have gathered together, as a hen gathereth her chickens." No compassion is there greater than that of the hen to her chicks. How did he in the foresight of her miseries approaching, Luke 19, weep over her, and cry, "O that

thou hadst known." The high Priest was therefore to be taken from among men, that he might have compassion on them that were ignorant and out of the way (Heb. 5:2). Is there any object in the world that deserves more pity than a lost soul, in the snare of the devil, blessing itself as if it were well, when it is poor, blind, beggarly, and naked, and every hour liable to an insufferable, an eternal destruction?

3. Thirdly, we must preach convincingly. First, there must be evidence of reason convincing the understanding of that we would persuade men to. Man is a reasonable creature, not drawn here and there by a thunder and lightning of blustering terms, which at the utmost only startle the affections for a time, but afterwards for lack of a convicted judgement they return to their old temper. In Col. 2:2, this is that which is called, the full assurance of understanding.

2. There is also required a conviction of the conscience, by which we evidence to men, that they are guilty, convincing them that they are the men. That was it that vexed the priests, that the Apostle taxed them in particular, (Acts 5:28, 33), as guilty of the blood of Christ, "He intends to bring this man's blood upon us." The Jews that stoned Steven, (Acts 1:35), were cut to the

heart, when he charged them in particular as stiff-necked and uncircumcised in heart. Men will endure much if you let them alone, or in the practice of their sins, but if they are apprehensive that your reproofs come home to them, they then are stained and filled with wrath, (Luke 4:28; 1 Cor. 14:25). When the preacher is manifest in the conscience of the hearers, then they confess that God is in him, they cry out, *Omnis actio fit per contractum.* You prophecy evil to us, (1 King 22:8). As the Philosophers say, that all action is by touching, so all doctrine works by particular *application;* he that delivers himself altogether in generals, seldom works on the people.[49] It is the spreading of the net (which is done by particular application) which takes the fish; always provided that we must not decipher men by personal circumstances or distinguishing characters. This will take off the efficacy of our reproof, in that the reproved will question the good affection of the reprover, as not tendering his good name, while he does that openly, which should have been done secretly. Only, if any man's sin, or a known circumstance of his sin discovers him, it is not the reprover, but the offender that discovers

---

[49] Ab usu doctrina ad ejus applicationem descensus est quidam quasi a specie ad individuu transitus. Zeppar. *de habend.* Concio.

himself. Sins must not be passed over in silence which declare themselves, because men complain that we particularize.

4. Fourthly, we must preach feelingly according to the nature of the doctrine; we do so when we preach as sensible in our own hearts of what we would have taken as an impression on another. The best way to speak to the heart, is to speak from the heart. Saint Paul when he would beget in the Corinthians a godly sorrow of heart, (2 Cor. 2:4), he writes to them out of much affliction and anxiety of spirit, with many tears. He that will make men sensible of wrath and damnation, or make men apprehensive of the greatness of God's love in Christ, must manifest the same affections in himself. There are many (Calvin says) clamorous preachers, who declaiming, or rather thundering against other men's faults, carry a great show of zeal, and in the meanwhile are very secure themselves, as if they did only sportingly exercise their throats and sides.[50] But a godly pastor must weep himself, that he may stir up compassion in others, and retain more sorrow in himself than he seeks to create in others.

---

[50] Calv: in loc.

5. Fifthly, when we preach frequently taking all occasions to dispense the Word; the Apostle calls it, in season, and out of season. The people's incapableness, their slowness to believe, their aptness to be carried away with the torrent of the times, the many ways by which the Word may miscarry; all these, besides the important nature of the work, as tending to bring men from the power of Satan to God, from hell to heaven, call for our redoubled pains. How constant and assiduous are merchants, mariners, husbandmen, in their attendance on their earthly affairs, which notwithstanding they ordinarily find as they left them? Should not we be much more industrious in soul-work, which we seldom or never return to it but we find it worse than we left it? Of the Lord's watchmen it is said, "That they shall not hold their peace all the day nor all the night," (Isaiah 62:6). Of Christ it is said, he was daily in the Temple teaching, (Luke 21:37), of the Apostles, that they were daily in the Temple, and from house to house preaching the Gospel, (Acts 5:42). The diligence

of the Ancients, as Chrysostom,[51] Basil,[52] Augustine,[53] the custom of the Church of which Eusebius reports,[54] ought to be as incitements to us. If John Hooper Bishop of Gloucester, in a confession of faith, exhibited to King Edward VI, says, "Masses in a day was not enough for the Popish Priests, shall one sermon suffice us?" he asked. "In the morning sow thy seed, and in the evening withhold not thine hand: for thou knowest not whether shall prosper, either this or that, or whether they both shall be alike good," (Eccl. 11:6).

6. Sixthly, we must preach gravely, so as to preserve the honor of that God whose mouth we are in preaching, of that Christ whose person we represent, of the high nature of the things we treat about (2 Cor. 5). We are to deal with men, and that in the presence of God and his holy angels, about their recovery out of their damnable condition by nature, in setting out the infinite love of God in Christ, with all the advantages that belong to it, the souls salvation or destruction to all

---

[51] Chrys. Hom. 3 in *Gen. Hom. 10.* in *Gen. Hom 9.* ad Pop. Antioch.
[52] Basil. *Hexem Hom 2.* ad finem. *Hom. 7.* Iam advesperascit, etc. (It seems they preached in the afternoon.)
[53] Aug. in *Tract. 9.* Hesternoenim die distulimus in hodiernum. Where it appears he preached daily. Vid. etiam *Tractat. 16.21.22.* alibi.
[54] Eusch. *de Praepar. Evang.* l. 8. c. 2. nus de senioribus legem recitat per totum diem septimum, as. usque ad vespertinum crepusculum.

eternity. How ill does anything that is ludicrous tending to move laughter have any place in discourses of so high a nature? All our care should be to preserve the spirits of men in a serious temper, in which they are fittest to be worked on. All laughter in the church is from the devil Chrysostom says. Funny stories are from this ground to be banished from the pulpit. A minister must be an example to the people in all gravity, (Titus 2:8), and this gravity must appear as in our whole conversation, so specially when we stand between God and the people as his ambassadors.

And now having represented to you, my Reverend Brethren, the important and pressing nature of your work, laid before you those general duties, by which you may be fitted and made successful in the work, set on those duties by quickening motives; what remains but that I commend you to God, and the Word of his grace who alone must enable you for it, and without whom all is done will come to nothing. And for you, our Parliamentary Worthies, you are (as things stand) under God the breath of our nostrils, the light of our eyes, as a nailed fastened (as yet) in a sure place; if you go on to do the Lord's work with wisdom and courage, God will certainly go along with you. If you refuse or withdraw yourselves (however our eyes shall be to the Lord, but) in the eye of man we are but an undone Nation. The God of heaven who has his way in the seas, who alone fashions the hearts of the children of men, raise and keep up your spirits, clothe you with zeal, fit you for all encounters, make way for you through all difficulties. So shall our religion, our laws, and liberties, be preserved to ourselves, and transmitted to posterity; and we have cause to praise God for you so long as the sun and the moon endures.

FINIS.

Other Works by Westminster Divines on Reformation Published by Puritan Publications

Reformation and Desolation
by Stephen Marshall (1594–1655)

Are you expecting to see God move in reforming the church? Why? Is your heart settled to continue the work of reformation? Are you truly expecting biblical revival?

The Christian's Duty Towards Reformation
by Thomas Ford (1598–1674)

Are you ready for Reformation to occur? Thomas Ford says that you must not only be ready for it to occur, but that you must be settled to see it through to the end. This is EVERY Christian's duty before God daily. Ford masterfully deals with Josiah's reformation, and why it did not last through to the end after the King's death. This is truly an important work on discerning the manner in which God will bless true biblical reformation.

The Precious Seeds of Reformation
by Humphrey Hardwicke (n.d.)

How willing are you to be used of God for the work of Reformation? Is reforming the church precious to you? Such work is hard, and often in the midst of being hated and ridiculed, even by complacent Christians in the church. In this rare puritan work, Hardwicke explains how our sowing in tears will ultimately, in God's timing, be filled with reaping in joy. We are not to live in doubt of God's work of providence for the good of his people!

A Discourse on Church Discipline and Reformation
by Daniel Cawdrey (1588-1664)

Are you your brother's keeper? Christians and Pastors alike should read Daniel Cawdrey's excellent work on church discipline and entrance to the sacrament of communion. A must read in our day where censure is all but lost.

Family Reformation Promoted, and Other Works
by Daniel Cawdrey (1588-1664)

How reformed is your family? Daniel Cawdrey has taken William Gouge's work, "Domestical Duty" and made it usable for today's reader. An awesome puritan work which includes three other never before published works of Cawdrey.

Gradual Reformation Intolerable
by C. Matthew McMahon and Anthony Burgess (1600-1663)

Is there a need for a biblical reformation today? The answer on that is a Bible-thumping YES! But should it happen slowly and gradually? Was this the method Christ used in preaching, or the Reformers? McMahon and Burgess team up to give the thoughtful Christian a biblical foundation to promote current reformation in their church and their homes.

The Difficulties of and Encouragements to a Reformation
by Anthony Burgess (1600-1663) 2nd Ed.

How hard is it for Reformation to take place? How hard is it for YOUR personal reformation to occur? This is a wonderful treatise on Mark 1:2-3 that shows how hard it is for true reformation to take place. Burgess encourages us toward reformation nonetheless.

www.ingramcontent.com/pod-product-compliance
Lightning Source LLC
Chambersburg PA
CBHW032132090426
42743CB00007B/568